GET A GRIP!

On your Authentic Self –

A Step-by-Step Guide to Personal Success

Renate Weiler

ExecutiveMentors Publishing

1111 Davis Drive, Unit 1 – Suite 178
Newmarket, ON L3Y 7V1
905-830-1985

ISBN 0-9733045-0-2
Printed and bound in Canada

Cover Design by:	Joanne van Hoof Xplore Designs joannevh@ica.net 905-847-3811
Editing by:	Carole Green seagreen@sympatico.ca 905-715-8819
Illustrated by:	Caroline Holroyd 905-953-8339
Text Design by:	Candi Lewis Vivid Designs vividdesigns@rogers.com 705-446-9760
Proofed by:	Dianne Moon Dianne Moon & Associates dianne@diannemoon.com 905-473-2492

National Library of Canada Cataloguing in Publication
Weiler, Renate
Get A Grip, on Your Authentic Self; editing by Carole Green

ISBN 0-9733045-0-2
1. Self-Actualization (Psychology). I. Title.
BF637.S8W35 2003 158.1 C2003-902664-7

CONTENTS

FOREWORD

Within your hands you hold the key to your luminous future. Everything you need is within you now and Get a Grip will show you how to bring out the very best that is within you.

As you go through each and every page of this powerful and life-changing book, allow the wisdom to permeate your soul. Reveal to the world the greatness that is within you. Remember that this greatness is not reserved for a select few – it is within everyone! You included.

Do not let old limiting beliefs stop you from following through. Make a commitment to step beyond your comfort zones and stretch yourself. When you stretch yourself, you will grow. This is where the miracles begin.

Many years ago I heard the saying (and I'm paraphrasing) "No amount of reading, listening to tapes, or going to seminars will bring you riches. It is the understanding and application of wise thoughts that makes the difference." Renate Weiler has created a masterpiece with Get a Grip that is simple, easy to understand and more important, easy to apply.

You will reach new heights that you only previously dreamed of when you follow Renate's magnificent suggestions. Make a commitment to yourself, right now, this very moment, that you will, not only read this book, you will devour it. You will eat it up like a hungry bear. Take this book on as if your life depended on it...because you may be surprised, that it actually does.

Purchasing this book demonstrates a phenomenal investment in yourself and in your future. You now have the tool within your hands to create an extraordinary life. Make your life something that is more than just long.

Peggy McColl
www.destinies.com

DEDICATION

I dedicate this inspiration to the three wonderful men in my life...

Fritz – you showered me with unconditional love
when I least expected to be loved.

Matt – every day your enthusiasm encourages
me to hold onto my vision.

Alex – your resolve and conviction is a source of joy to me.

Thank you for loving me and believing in my vision.

ACKNOWLEDGEMENTS:

John and Shirley Bowerbank for entrusting me with the treasures of your heart, taking me under your wings and expecting me to win. Thank you for raising the bar for me, encouraging me to do more, take bigger steps and believe in myself.

Peggy McColl for generously sharing your wisdom, contacts and skills. Your enthusiasm for this book added excitement and gave me the courage to step out on the limb even further.

Debbie Philp, my friend who always believed that this inspiration needed to be published.

Carole Green, my editor for allowing my own voice to be heard and gently channelling my exuberance into a polished format.

Francine Hoffman, my business mentor and friend, whose positive expectations always bring out the best in me.

Sean Herbinson for your unwavering belief in me. You have been a source of strength and hope.

Leslie Traill – your insights and wisdom have guided me well.

Eva Elo because with your virtual help, I could do anything.

Joanne van Hoof for your creativity and patience. Working with you was a joy.

Caroline Holroyd for capturing my visions perfectly in all of the illustrations.

Executive Mentors members because your dedication and support fueled my inspiration.

Sandra and Kym Yancey for taking me into your hearts and offering me "the" opportunity. Thank you for believing that I could make you proud and represent you well in Canada.

eWomenNetwork members for your generosity in sharing your contacts with me. You made publishing this book a pleasant journey.

Success team 2002: Donna Messer, Jennifer Beale, Theresa Chan, JoAnne Fleming, Cathy Nesbitt, Nina Menezes, Richard Messer, Rena Anderson, Sharon DeSousa, Brenda Langendoen, Sylvia O'Brien, Rena Anderson – for without your support and encouragement, this publication would still be a dream, hiding in the recesses of my mind.

Thank you to all of my family, friends, business associates and supporters. You added spice and excitement to my days. I am grateful to have met all of you and to have travelled along the path with you.

Enjoy your journeys!

THE BUZZ ABOUT "GET A GRIP"

"A masterpiece! Simple, easy to apply and powerful! Follow Renate's guidelines and you will be thrilled with the level of success that you will reach."

Peggy McColl, Author of The 8 Proven Secrets to SMART Success and On Being a Dog with a Bone.

"Renate's perspective changed my life, opened doors galore…launching a rocket that I now know as my thriving new personal business. I 'got a grip', Oh, boy did I! And it is something that I wish for all of her readers. When you work through this book and really accept the loving voice with which it was written, you can't help but come to the final page a beautifully evolved human being."

Carole E. McGill-Green, Writer

"Wow, I love this book! Succinct, easy to follow, informative and empowering. A wonderful tool to understand oneself better and move forward in quantum leaps.

Leslie Traill, Meditation Coach and Astrological Consultant

"Fantastic, to the point and easy to digest.

Francine Hoffman, Francine Hoffman Organization

"A must read for everyone. This book has given me a feeling of power, the courage to take control and move forward, toward my goals. I now understand, that the little bumps on my path of growth are just obstacles placed there by my own fears and insecurities. I now can "Get a Grip" on my big, huge and audacious goals and create my reality."

Deborah Philp, Natural Health Care Practitioner – Iridologist

"Splendid, can't wait to review "Get A Grip" for my readers at BWC magazine."

Donna Messer, Managing Editor of BWC magazine, and President of Connect Us Communications, Canada

INTRODUCTION

The beautiful people, the crème de la crème of society, are admired by many and seen to be wealthy and happy. Their opulent lifestyles seem unattainable for most average folks. Yet, many would say that these luxurious lifestyles are just what we would love to experience, "if only" we had been born into a privileged family.

Chasing the elusive dream of a fabulous lifestyle has reduced us to purchasing lottery tickets on a weekly basis, encouraging our imagination to play the "what if" or the "imagine the freedom" game. (Only a few fleeting moments of fantasy followed by a crash back into the harsh reality of our own lives once the winning numbers have been announced).

Some of us observe the physically beautiful among us and think that "if only" we had been blessed in such a way, our lives would be perfect and we would be happy at last. Why does the "grass always seem to look greener" in the neighbours yard?

If you have come to a point in your life where you are questioning why you are where you are and feeling the way that you do, this book is for you. However, it is not meant to replace professional counselling nor is it a 'quick fix' for deep-seated emotional challenges. For those of you who find yourself stuck in a rut, working through the pages of this book and answering all of the questions as they come up can assist you to change your life and get on track to the life that you dream of. The worksheets and questions herein are intended to be helpful tools that will aid you to 'get a grip' on your life, guiding you along an exciting path toward a future designed by you for yourself with purpose and life-giving energy.

I hope you will find your journey as rewarding as I have found my own. Make yourself comfortable, have a pen ready, sit back, relax and travel with me toward your future.

Begin by signing below, thereby making a very important commitment to yourself to "work" through this book. Answer the questions as and when they are presented, honestly and to the best of your ability.

I, ________________________ , am ready to "Get a Grip" on my life!

Signed: ________________________ dated: ____________________

"No wind favours him who has not a destined port!"
...Montaigne

CHAPTER 1

JOURNEY TO TODAY

"Seventeen years old and hair of gold" was a hugely successful love song in Germany in the late 1960's. I was 17 years old, had blond hair, and stood 6' tall weighing no less than 275 pounds. I loved that song, yet it caused me pain and anguish to listen to those lovely words. I certainly did not feel that I was loved as the song suggested.

The question "How did I get here?" never occurred to me then. Instead, "Why me?" was the thought that occupied most of my waking moments. Every aspect of my life was measured against an unrealistic utopist ideal thus doomed to failure. I don't recall even one moment when I felt happy. In fact, I remember feeling desperately alone and utterly hopeless. Linda Ronstat's song "Poor, poor pitiful me" perfectly described my late teen years.

WHICH SONG TITLE WOULD SUMMARIZE WHERE YOU ARE AT RIGHT NOW?

THE GOOD, THE BAD AND THE UGLY GOALS

Ideally, goals are similar to guided missiles, propelling us toward a specific point in time when we will accomplish a task or achieve a dream. Good goals, properly designed, thought through and executed, will indeed take us into the future that we dream about. However, there are also goals which I refer to as the bad and the ugly goals. Poorly thought out and designed, they can interrupt our lives, stealing our dreams and hopes.

In Chapter 2, we will design good goals by carefully thinking through the action plan. Then, using the proper tools, we will enable ourselves to be propelled into a superb future. But for now, let's look at why the bad and ugly goals are destructive, stealing our dreams, dashing our hopes for a better future.

I started to set goals during the darkest time of my young life – in my late teens. To be more precise, one goal and one goal only consumed me. "Losing weight". Notice that I didn't say "becoming healthy" or "reaching my target weight sensibly" – but "losing weight" no matter what, regardless of how. Willing to pay any price for this 'sure ticket to happiness', I embarked on a dieting program that (but for the grace of God) should have killed me or left me with severe health challenges. I don't ever share how I dropped 80 pounds because I know there is a person reading this book right now who may be willing to risk their life for such a significant weight loss no matter what the cost. However, this book is intended to enhance lives as opposed to destroying them, so I shall keep to myself the nature of my ugly 'recipe' for weight loss.

NAME ONE UGLY GOAL THAT IS YOUR DAILY COMPANION:

____

"No person was ever honoured for what they received. Honour has been the reward for what they gave."...Calvin Coolidge

NO FREE LUNCH!

Working towards a goal requires sacrifices. A price has to be paid even for a bad or ugly goal – without exception. That certainly was true for me. I sacrificed healthy family relationships by blaming others for my unhappiness and excessive weight. Looking back now, I can clearly see how I had taken leave of my sanity, giving up joy and losing touch with my delicious sense of humor. Losing self while pursuing "the ugly goal" proved to be expensive. At the time, I was not aware that I would eventually have to pay back this emotional loan. The actual cost of my ugly goal grew exponentially over the years and added up to a much heftier price tag than I could have ever imagined.

WHAT DID YOU HAVE TO SACRIFICE OR PAY FOR YOUR BAD/UGLY GOAL?

____

____

____

"The thing always happens that you really believe in, and the belief in a thing makes it happen." ...Frank Lloyd Wright

"THE TRUTH COULD BE A LIE"

The most powerful tool we all possess is our thoughts. Thoughts have energy and, like magnets, they propel us toward that which we think about the most. You have probably heard it said many times before that "what you believe, you can achieve". As a general rule, individuals seldom exceed their own expectations. Often we are unaware that, on a subconscious level, we are constantly working to live up to what we truly believe about ourselves. Thoughts are born out of our beliefs.

Becoming aware of our thoughts gives us an insight into our beliefs, which influence every decision that we make and every action that we take. Listen carefully to your thoughts! You might just surprise yourself.

WHICH THOUGHT IS MOST DOMINANT IN YOUR MIND ON A DAILY BASIS?

Without a shadow of a doubt, I believed that if only I could be skinny, I would be happy and life would be wonderful, glorious...absolutely perfect. Surely then people would love me, enjoy my company and I would experience peace of mind while living a life of luxury, excitement and adventure. Imagine my surprise, after having lost 80 pounds, to learn that my life had not improved. (Unless you count the initial but short-lived onslaught of compliments). This harsh reality, this total 'unfairness' sent me straight back to my friend, "food". For the next few decades my love/hate relationship with food and dieting would be my constant companion. I gained and lost enough weight to make up whole families, even small villages. At a point, I concluded that goal setting just did not work because when I arrived at my goal, I did not get my prize. Many years would pass before I was willing to adjust my view of goal setting.

WHAT DO YOU BELIEVE WILL HAPPEN WHEN YOU REACH YOUR UGLY GOAL? (if you have one)

"It is not my aptitude but my attitude that determines my altitude."…Reverend Jessie Jackson

ATTITUDE IS EVERYTHING

The sign in front of the financial consultant's office read: "Attitude is everything – pick a good one". Habits of thought that control our spontaneous actions are what we commonly refer to as attitudes. On the subconscious level we lean either towards or away from something – like or dislike something or someone.

Personally, I always did have a positive attitude – I was positive that I was right all of the time! Little did I know that my need to be right was rooted in very low self-esteem and poor self-image. How could I be expected to feel warmly toward the fat person that I saw in the mirror every day? Of course, every time I looked into the mirror, that reflection of a "fat me" perpetuated my poor self-image because I simply could not look past the extra weight. This contorted and negative self-image stayed with me even when I finally weighed in at a healthy, ideal body weight. It took years for me to accept the new me.

YOUR ATTITUDE ABOUT YOUR LIFE AND YOURSELF IS:

"Faith is not the contradiction of reality, it is facing the reality with hope and courage."...Dr. Robert Schuller

FAITH IS A KEY INGREDIENT

When I was a child, Sunday was my favourite day of the week. I got to go to church by myself, listen to beautiful music, ignore the ministers preaching, and imagined myself with my creator, feeling loved, comfortable and accepted – such bliss! As a child, I prayed often – usually when I was in big trouble and wanted to avoid punishment. My prayers, though, were never answered.

Yet, I held onto my faith over the years. I always believed that I had been created by God and in his image. I also believed that I had let God down (by not being perfect and all). Throughout my life journey I have, at times, struggled with my personal faith and how to express it in my day-to-day life. Thankfully, my struggles have made me stronger and taught me valuable lessons, which I can now share with you as well as the participants at my seminars, workshops and my image clients.

When my oldest son was fairly young, he offered to build me a time machine so I could go back to an earlier time in my life and fix the errors that I had made along the way. His thinking was that this would make my present life much easier. His offer touched me. Often I would tell him how lucky he was. Although he didn't know much about my life, he did seem to understand that my saying this suggested that I had not been so fortunate. (A very compassionate child you might say.) I assured him that I believed he would one day build that fabulous machine, but that he need not do it for me. He couldn't understand why I would refuse this wonderful opportunity for a happier life.

To make my point, I told him the story about how a caterpillar becomes a butterfly. I explained that the would-be butterfly finds itself in a cocoon and its natural instinct compels it to break free of the confinement of the cocoon. It has to work hard to break through the walls if it ever wants to become a butterfly. The struggle is tough and leaves the insect exhausted.

A spectator might be tempted to offer a helping hand by cracking the cocoon open for the new butterfly. Yet only through the struggle to freedom will the wings of the butterfly become strong enough to take flight! Struggle is so very necessary for all creatures in order that they can experience a sense of freedom and success.

I wanted my son to understand that, if it had not been for the struggles in my life, I would not have become the person that I am today. I believe that he has never offered the time machine again because he likes me fine just the way I am (and so do I).

Through my personal struggles I have held onto my faith in my God, knowing that I am created for greatness and to love others as he has loved me – unconditionally. I have learned that, although I am only one person, I can touch many by sharing my thoughts, improving myself and keeping up my prayer life. We don't all believe in the same God or perhaps any God at all, yet we can benefit greatly by believing that we are part of a greater creation.

HOW DO YOU EXPRESS YOUR FAITH ON A DAILY BASIS?

____

____

____

____

____

CHAPTER 2

CREATING A GREAT TOMORROW

Recognizing that we are not in life where we think we should be is a simple task for most people. Knowing what we do not like comes easily to us, yet pinpointing where we would rather be is much more difficult to ascertain. Our dislikes are due to involuntary emotional responses telling us that something does not feel right – because it doesn't make us feel happy. Happiness is often used as a yardstick to measure how well we are mastering the competitive game called 'Life'.

"Most folks are about as happy as they make their minds up to be."…Abraham Lincoln

GETTING YOUR SLICE OF THE PIE

Popular opinion, supported by the media, has many convinced that, when we have all the right kind of possessions, we will finally be happy. Living in the right neighbourhood, driving the car of our dreams and working in a prestigious profession means we have won the competition and now have the right to be happy. Is it any wonder then that many are working so very hard to earn their slice of happiness?

My mother's voice still rings in my ears to this day. Confronted with my constant moaning about my lack of happiness, she would exclaim with exasperation in her voice, *"Why can't you just be happy?"* This comment (coming from a woman who lived her life guided by duty) made me shake my head. I wondered what she could possibly know about the blissful state of happiness?

My theory was that, once I had the right 'stuff' and got to be happy, then that blissful state of mind would be mine forever. Mine, each and every second of every day! Instead, I only experienced glimpses of happiness ever so infrequently, when opening a gift or receiving acknowledgement for a job well done. As quickly as a fragment of happiness came into my awareness, it disappeared again. The elusiveness of happiness was annoying because I could not figure out how to hold on to it and make it mine for good. For years, I believed that happiness was a bit like the grace of God, bestowed upon just a few lucky ones (and some of them certainly seemed undeserving). How very unfair indeed.

WHAT DOES IT TAKE FOR YOU TO FEEL HAPPY?

____

Many years later I realized that the 'Grace of God' is given to all who accept it. Happiness works much the same way. It turned out that my Mom was right after all. Happiness is a decision; one we make each and every day anew. Accepting where we are at right now in our lives and moving fearlessly towards our good goals is, in essence, making the decision to be happy.

How can you get your share? Decide and choose to be happy. That is all it takes. As Abraham Lincoln said, *"Most folks are just about as happy as they make up their minds to be"*. All of us have a God given right to choose happiness, but making the decision to do so is our own responsibility.

Complete this sentence:
I AGREE TO TAKE RESPONSIBILITY FOR:

____

Our potential is unlimited, yet it can be imprisoned by our own fears, disbeliefs and resistance to change. Taking responsibility is not a punishment but rather an awesome opportunity to become the captain of the ship called 'Life', setting course toward our very own ideal future.

"The future belongs to those who believe in their dreams."...Eleanor Roosevelt

DREAMING BIG, HUGE AND AUDACIOUS DREAMS

Wishes are like sandcastles built on the beach during a hot summer day. They are easily washed away by the waves of the incoming tide. "I wish I were", "I wish I had", "I wish I could" are thoughts preceding fantasies and daydreams. Lying awake until the early morning hours, creating my fantasy life was one of my favourite past times. Wonderful hours spent imagining a beautiful and happy life – only to be faced with the reality of my world the next morning. I continually found myself to be both tired and profoundly disappointed, for my reality had not magically changed over night. Wishes, like candy floss, have no substance. They may look pretty and taste sweet but they cannot satisfy real hunger.

WHICH WISH KEEPS POPPING INTO YOUR MIND?

____

Good goals, unlike wishes, do have substance and can satisfy a deep-seated hunger, a true desire. Good goals are magical indeed because they have the power to propel us toward a desired future, energizing us and exciting us as nothing else can. To the uninitiated and those disappointed by life, goals can also seem unreal or even scary. It certainly is easier to wish for a wonderful life and lose ourselves in a fantasy world than it is to goal-set for a wonderful life, becoming responsible for making it happen.

The lack of good goals reduces us to a state of helplessness. Circumstances and other people's agendas twist and twirl us around like a boat without a sail in the rough waters of life. Success and achievement are left to the whim of chance rather than to a plan with a purpose. Frustrated by the numerous misses that chance holds in store, many have resigned themselves to an unsatisfying routine life.

Believing that goal setting just doesn't work for them, they often choose to live vicariously through a steady diet of "Reality Shows" offered up by the media.

Presenting "Life Skill Seminars" at correctional facilities in Western Canada allowed me the opportunity to encourage young people to "Get a Grip" on their lives. They learned to make positive changes using a goal setting technique that works marvelously. This technique, that I am about to share with you, is different from any other that you may have tried, heard or read about. However, it requires your willingness to keep an open mind. A mind, similar to a parachute, works best when it is open. Discovering your good goals and crystallizing them is a very personal journey, unique to each individual. It requires your complete focus and attention. Identifying what your innermost spirit and soul truly wants is the key to successful goal setting. It energizes and excites.

If you have had experience with relaxation or meditation techniques, this will be a simple step for you to take. For those not having had the opportunity to participate in such an exercise before, simply read the instructions several times until you understand exactly what you need to do and then allow yourself to relax. A taped version of the instructions can be ordered, or you can create your own tape with soft background music. My favourite music for this exercise is a variety of soft classical pieces of music by Steven Halpern. Make sure that you are in a quiet, comfortable spot where you won't be disturbed for the next hour. Read the instructions several times until you understand exactly what you need to do and then allow yourself to relax. Some soft music in the background helps you relax more quickly. Let us begin:

Your eyes are closed, you are breathing in slowly and deeply through your nose, holding on to the air in your lungs for a few seconds and then slowly exhaling through slightly opened lips. Repeat this as many times as is necessary for you to feel relaxed. Focus your attention on different parts of your body, sending the message of relaxation to each of them. Start with your feet. Think, "My feet are relaxing"...pause…"relaxing"... pause... "relaxed". Work your way up the body. Now your entire body is relaxed.

Imagine yourself walking along a path in a forest. The weather is beautiful. Everything around you is absolutely perfect and you feel wonderful. Look around and take in the glorious scenery. Smell the fragrance of wildflowers growing along side of the path. Become aware of sounds surrounding you… birds singing, squirrels rustling through the leaves, rabbits foraging for food. You are totally relaxed. You feel at peace with yourself.

Through the bright sunshine, a person is approaching you. Without so much as a verbal exchange, you instinctively know that they are glad to see you and that the feeling is mutual. You recognize the individual as a very much older version of yourself. The older 'you' invites you to change places, so that you can have an opportunity to see what your life has become after so many years have passed. Gladly, you accept the offer, knowing that you will reclaim your younger self shortly. Trust yourself to know where you have to go and in your mind's eye see yourself having arrived at your future home. Look around and observe where you are. If you can't recognize the location, don't fret. Just tell yourself that you will have perfect recall later when you'll write down everything you saw, heard, and simply knew to be true. Answer these questions in your mind. Who are the people around you? What are they doing? Your home reminds you of...? Observe how the home is decorated. Where is your favourite spot? Go to that area and see why it is so special to you. Recognize the fabulous treasures that this room reveals to you. Here you see evidence of a life filled with accomplishments, dreams realized and goals surpassed. Spend time here and discover what you are most proud of in a life well lived. You now know, without a doubt, what your life was all about, who you really were meant to be all along. Stay until you have a clear picture of this future embedded in your mind, knowing you'll remember it all after you have opened your eyes again. Soak in this wonderful life and the great memories that linger here. When you are ready, return to the path. As you are walking away from this place, know that real time has not yet past and the course you choose from now on is entirely up to you.

You meet up with your other self, exchanging places. Have a good look at the older you as you are saying your good-byes. Drink in the loving gaze of the 'older you' that promises peace, joy and a sense of purpose which is ready to be claimed by you in your near future. Travel the path back through the forest and rest a little while before deciding to return to a state of full awareness. You'll feel energized, alive and joyful. Breathe in deeply through the nose and allow your eyelids to open slightly. Close your eyes again for a few seconds. Repeat this until you feel comfortable to open your eyes fully. Eyes wide open now, stand up and stretch your legs.

Write down everything you saw, heard, observed and felt without analyzing any of the information. Nothing is to be left out; even the smallest detail needs to be recorded on the following pages. If you need more paper than provided, get some more and keep writing.

From the information that you have already written down, answer the following questions:

What struck you most about the 'older you'?

Where was your future place? Describe.

What type of landscape did you notice?

If there were other people there, who were they? If you didn't recognize them, how did they seem to you?

What type of home did you visit?

Where was your special place? Describe.

What did you notice most about your surroundings?

Which were the treasures that were revealed to you?

What did you see, realize or sense was your greatest accomplishment?

What would you say you had been most proud of as the 'older you'?

____

____

____

Based on your observations, what was most important to you?

____

____

____

What did you see in your special space that surprised you?

____

____

____

Describe what you saw that you would really like to have but don't have yet:

____

____

____

____

CHAPTER 3

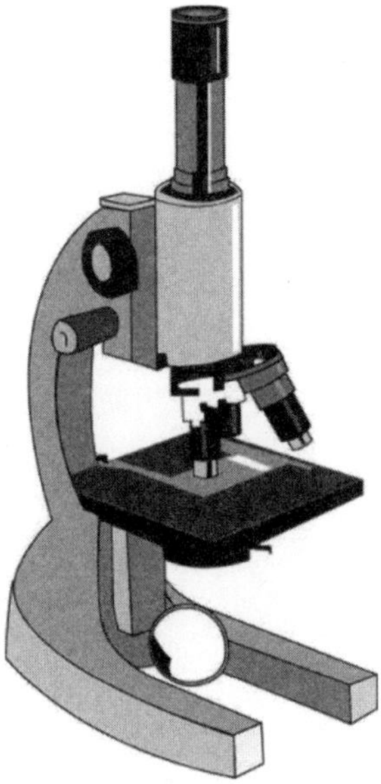

"Our lives improve only when we take chances – and the first and most difficult risk we can take is to be honest with ourselves."... Walter Anderson

INSIGHTS FROM THE JOURNEY

Knowing what we want to accomplish is the first step to getting a grip on our life, emotions and actions. You have, by answering the questions in the last chapter, taken that crucial step. If this truly is the life that you desire, then let's get started in plotting a course of action designed to bring your future into the realm of reality. Maybe you are already heading in the right direction and just need a slight adjustment to make things happen or to speed up the process. Let's find out.

HONESTY COMES FIRST

If you continue doing what you have been doing, will your present actions eventually take you to your big, huge, audacious goal?

❍ YES ❍ NO

Yes? Wonderful. Let's speed up the process. Go on to 'Positives'.

No? Okay then! Let's get busy developing a plan of action, focussing on the goals and putting into place the future you that you have designed. A person living your big, huge, audacious goal would have:
These skills/knowledge:

____

____

These attitudes/beliefs:

____

____

Take these actions:

____

____

What skills, knowledge, attitudes, beliefs and actions have you written down that you do not yet have, or perhaps need to strengthen? Circle those and write them into the following table:

Presently missing, or needing work:

____

____

Are you willing to do whatever it takes to learn the needed skills, acquire the missing knowledge, develop appropriate attitudes and beliefs and take the necessary actions? Because you have been reading and writing this far, you have shown yourself that you are really serious about working toward the future designed and envisioned by you. Commit to taking courses that teach the missing skills and knowledge. Life Coaches, Business Coaches and Mentors are wonderful resources when looking for one-on-one guidance in the attitudes, beliefs and actions. Most successful individuals I know have accessed such resources and readily admit their success is due to their willingness to make themselves accountable to a mentor.

Complete the following sentences:

I commit to learn ________________________ by registering for

__________________________________ course, to be completed

by ________________.

____

Signature + date

I commit to becoming accountable to: ________________________

(a person I respect)

____

Signature + date

Becoming accountable to somebody else tends to help us in staying focussed on our goals. It encourages us to pursue them vigorously under the guidance of a mentor - a person we respect and trust.
Your relationship with a mentor needs to be open, honest and positive.

This is not to say that your mentor will love all you do, but you will be able to count on them to communicate in a constructive manner, coaching you towards your goals and commitments. Choosing a mentor is a process that requires you to interview several people for the position. You will not only want to make certain that your personalities click, but also that your mentor is successful in the areas you want to work on. Be prepared to pay for his or her service and be willing to make at least a twelve month commitment to the mentoring process.

"Gratitude is born in the hearts that take time to count up past mercies."... Charles E. Jefferson

A PAT ON THE BACK

Often we take for granted the wonderful strengths we possess. Becoming aware of that which is great about us is essential in the process of achieving our big, huge, audacious goals. List all of your positive and powerful qualities:

____

____

____

____

____

Are you surprised by the many positive and powerful qualities you came up with? We tend to take so many things about ourselves for granted that much about our personal power stays hidden, even from ourselves. The following will allow you to tap into your subconscious knowledge and gain greater awareness into your own greatness.

Write down your most favourite, only one, in each of the following categories:

If money were no problem, my favourite HOME would be:

____

My favourite MOVIE is (specific one or type):

____

The ANIMAL I like the best is:

____

My all-time favourite BOOK is (specific title or type):

____

Of all the HOLIDAYS, my absolutely favourite one is:

____

The CAR of my dreams is:

____

My most favourite PERSON in the whole world is:

____

If I could VACATION anywhere, it would be in:

____

The type of MUSIC or specific SONG I love most is:

____

My most favourite ACTIVITY/HOBBIE is:

____

The WEATHER I love best is:

____

How you would describe each of your favourites? Find three positive adjectives, for each one of your favourites.

Example:
Home: Mansion – adjectives could be elegant, beautiful, spacious.

Have fun with this process and allow yourself to be creative. The same adjective may appear more than once. If you cannot find another one to take its place, then that is just fine.

Adjectives, describing your favourites in each category:

HOME: ____________________________________

MOVIE: ____________________________________

ANIMAL: ______________________________

BOOK: ______________________________

HOLIDAY: ______________________________

CAR: ______________________________

PERSON: ______________________________

VACATION: ______________________________

MUSIC/SONG: ______________________________

ACTIVITY/HOBBY: ______________________________

WEATHER: ______________________________

Underline one adjective in each category. Examples:

HOME – mansion	elegant	beautiful	generous
MOVIE – sci-fi	exciting	adventurous	visionary
ANIMAL – dog	trusting	loyal	honest

Complete this process for each of your favourites.
Sample positive adjectives: *active, attentive, animated, attractive, brave, beautiful, caring, daring, elegant, invigorating, healthy, generous, kind, loving, successful, polite, strong, selfless, smart, intelligent, open-minded, handsome, powerful, loyal, trustworthy, adventurous, confident, honest, committed, persistent, eager, willing, determined, nice, gorgeous, hard working, gentle…*

Copy all underlined adjectives into this table:
(You will need them for chapter 4)

"Most people are not successful in life unless they have known a certain amount of failure. What you can learn from failure is that you do survive, you can be hurt, but you are not dead...it is not the end. The pain will pass and you can go on to succeed the next time around."
...Dr. Daniel Casriel – Casriel Institute, New York City

YOUR ACHILLES HEEL

Most people have set goals at one time in their lives and yet, somehow they managed not to reach their lofty ideals. Rather than giving up on goal-setting all together, let us find out what is or who is sabotaging your valiant efforts. In previous situations, what stopped you from reaching a goal? Did you have the skills and knowledge needed to accomplish your tasks? Did you make a sincere commitment to your goals? Yes, you most likely did all of that. What else is there that could keep you from reaching goals that you are able, willing and determined to reach? Thoughts are powerful allies and strong opponents in our daily life. These are the laws that govern our thoughts.

- Thoughts are <u>real forces</u>. They are tools. They are energy.
  Think about a situation that will cause you to react on an emotional level, either positively or negatively. Thoughts are powerful, indeed.
- Your mind is just like a radio station sending and receiving thoughts 24 hours a day. Consciously or not, you are constantly broadcasting

what you are thinking about to others who then "get" what is going on for you on a subconscious level. In the exact same manner, you are 'receiving' their thoughts.

- The law of attraction. Emotionalized thoughts become magnetized and attract similar thoughts. What we think about, we tend to draw into our own realm of reality. "Like attracts like".
- The law of control. We have the power and ability to either entertain or dismiss thoughts at any time we choose.
- The law of insertion. We can insert any thought of our choosing into our mind. This is a powerful privilege.
- The law of connection. Our inner and outer world is connected. We receive that which we most think about.

The greatest potential obstacle, keeping us from our desired future, is our very own thoughts. Nobody can stop us from reaching our goals once we have decided to go ahead and follow our chosen path. The mightiest enemy is the one within. Success or failure really is within our own reach.

We can choose and attain success by taking control of the six inch space between our very own ears – our thoughts. How many times have you talked yourself into something that may have seemed scary – outside of your comfort zone – yet you wanted it so badly that you talked yourself right through the terrifying aspects and then rejoiced in the success you were able to experience?

Talking to ourselves is verbalized thought. Thoughts are powerful. Verbalized thoughts are also called affirmations, cementing the words from our conscious into our subconscious. Reflect upon a time when you gave up on a goal and recall what you were thinking then.

What are you thinking now, while contemplating reaching for your big, huge, and audacious goal?

Becoming aware of the thoughts that are running through your mind right now will give you an indication as to what could be keeping you from your desired future. Are these thoughts similar to the ones that stopped you before? Are you ready and willing to break this pattern in your life? Write down the negative descriptions from those thoughts that stopped you before.

Usually we don't need help finding negatives, yet as I am not with you, here are some examples:

not smart enough…nobody in our family has ever…too tall, too short…no skills…money is not everything…who do I think I am?… I can't do this… I am not sure…I don't know…

Now take each negative and turn it around. In other words, write it as a positive statement.

____

____

____

____

For example:
not smart enough = "I am smart."
nobody in our family has ever = "I am the first in my family to …"
too tall, short = "I am just right the way I am."
no skills = "I am learning what it is that I need to know."
money is not everything = "The colour of money goes with everything I wear."
who do you think you are? = "I am special and unique."
I can't do this = "Yes, I can do everything I put my mind to accomplishing."
I am not sure = "I am certain and sure of myself."
I don't know = "I already know what I need to know."

Now that we know and understand how powerful thoughts are; that we can dismiss or entertain any thought of our choosing, then why not pick the thoughts that will take us to where we want to go? Challenges can either be roadblocks that keep us from our desired future or they can be opportunities to help us grow and become who we were meant to be. We do have the power to choose!

CHAPTER 4

GETTING FROM HERE TO THERE

If we have the power to choose, then how do we determine what changes need to be made? We already know that we want to arrive at our desired future – the goal that we identified in Chapter 2. We also have figured out where we are at right now – we discovered that as well in Chapter 2. Now, all we have left to do is bridge the gap.

"Seize the moment of excited curiosity on any subject to solve your doubts, for if you let it pass, the desire may never return, and you may remain in ignorance."... William Wirt

PLOTTING THE COURSE

In 'reality checks' you identified the skills and knowledge needed to accomplish your own big, huge and audacious goal. You have made the commitment to take care of that by taking courses, attending seminars and doing whatever it takes to gather the skills and necessary knowledge to fill those gaps. Now it is time to utilize all of those wonderful, positive adjectives you collected in the previous chapter. You wrote down your 'most favourite' in a variety of categories, then found three adjectives for each of those favourites to describe them. Out of each set of three adjectives, you kept one that really resonated with you.

Ideally, you might have eleven different, positive adjectives to work with in this chapter. We will also be using the statements from the 'laws of thought", where we took negative thoughts and turned them 'around' into positive statements. We are now ready to start filling the gaps.

You have, by now, recognized that in order to reach your big, huge and audacious goal, something will have to change within your own thought process. Just as I knew, when tipping the scale at 275 pounds, that (other than my pattern of food consumption) I had to change how I thought about and viewed myself. I could not expect to accomplish different results by doing the same things that I had always done. By becoming aware of these laws of thought, I recognized that I had found my starting point. I am suggesting that you are at your starting point right now! You can start changing your mind about yourself now. Let's begin by working on affirmations.

Affirmations are positively expressed statements of potential facts – manifestos of our hearts – prayers of our spirit. They can represent the gateway to the future that we desire. Many years ago, when I first met Mark Victor Hansen, he would address my doubts about succeeding as a professional speaker with these words:

"Renate, you have to fake it until you make it". But how could I pretend to be a great speaker if I was still nervous in front of an audience and struggling to get my message across? Mark assured me that the more I said "You have to fake it until you make it" to myself, the sooner I would become a great speaker. He told me that I also had to take the appropriate actions by continuing to perfect the skill.

Of course, I still thought that I was being dishonest by declaring that I was a great speaker, even though I only made this affirmation to myself. Amazingly, within months I noticed that my speeches sounded more polished. I felt less nervous and found that I had indeed bought into my own declarations.

When you first start your own declarations, you may hear your inner voice saying "yeah, but..." Simply recognize that voice to be your ever-present dissenter who wants to keep you within your own comfort zone. (Your comfort zone, by the way, isn't necessarily the zone that you want to be in but it is the place where you may feel competent and safe.)

Your declarations need to be written down, keeping these guidelines in mind:

- Each declaration pertains to only you. Affirm for yourself, not others.
- Affirm positive traits and characteristics.
- Write in the present tense, as though you already own it in reality.
- Indicate achievement, accomplishment – "I am, I have, I enjoy, I love"...
- Compare to your own best self – not to others.
- Use activity words such as: "I easily, I joyfully"... rather than words describing ability such as "I can"...
- Create excitement in your declarations: fun, happiness, pride, joy...
- Focus on accuracy and balance – do not sabotage yourself by over or undershooting.
- Affirm practical, realistic characteristics – not perfection.
- Remember to write your affirmations for yourself only.

Affirmations, declarations and manifestos are important catalysts to reaching goals. The words you are about to write down will trigger images in your mind and those will bring about emotions within you, consciously or unconsciously. This process will perpetuate the statements that you are making with these affirmations. Your mind is picture-oriented and, just like a guided missile, it will focus on and go after that for which it has been programmed. In other words, your mind will go after and bring to reality that which you affirm. Even though you may be affirming something that you have not yet bought into or believe to be possible, it will be drawn into your reality because the laws of thought pre-determined the outcome.

You are now ready to write out your declarations, using the positive statements and adjectives from the previous chapter. Just about now some of you might be thinking – "Just a minute here, some of the positive adjectives I wrote down are just not me". I certainly can relate to what you are feeling at this point. Years ago, when I completed the exercise in Chapter 3 about finding positive adjectives, the two that kept coming up for me were the words 'beautiful' and 'elegant'. When it came time to write my own affirmations, I quickly realized one of them would have to be along the lines of: *"I am beautiful and elegant."* At 275 pounds, that seemed to me to be a complete lie. I *knew* that I was neither beautiful nor elegant and so did everyone else who had ever met me. My goodness, how could I write such a lie on paper and pretend it was my truth? "Fake it until you make it" came echoing back from my memories.

A friend of mine, Jon Lee Kootnekoff, asked me the following questions to assist me in understanding my confusion. *"If you do not know what something looks like, how would you recognize it? If you have never had a feeling, how would you be able to describe it to somebody else?"*

Jon Lee is an inspiration to many and I admired him, yet his questions drove me beyond the point of reason. I believed that they had to be trick questions. I considered of all of the different angles I could use to come up with some answers that sounded right. However, eventually I had to surrender to the idea that I could only recognize or describe things and emotions that I knew first hand. That meant that deep inside, within my spirit I knew that I was beautiful and elegant, yet had willingly denied myself this precious knowledge. Living in denial had been easy for me because it allowed me to stay where little was expected of me. Better yet, if I did exceed those low expectations, I would be an immediate success (at least in my own mind). The beauty of this arrangement was that if I did not exceed the low expectations, I could always blame it on the excess weight. Oh, the days that I would spend dreaming about all of the wonderful things I would accomplish if it were not for the weight challenge! What a wonderful life I would lead. Poor, poor pitiful me. The elaborate games my mind managed to play! Most people, like myself, will eventually reach a point of quiet desperation where existing on a plane of low expectations and playing the 'blaming' game with a 'victim mentality' becomes too difficult, frustrating and exhausting. Something or somebody will do or say something to wake us up, shake us out of our stupor of unconsciousness and show us the path to a better life. My mentor, Jon Lee Kootnekoof, was just such a person and introduced me to the tools and skills needed to live a life of passion, excitement and high energy. I am grateful to him for risking being rebuked by me and for having the courage to be a true mentor by walking the path that he walked each and every day. It is my hope that this book is the catalyst for a life enhancing experience, taking you onto the path toward the future you desire.

The fact is, we can only see in others and in the world around us that which exists within ourselves already. Even if you still doubt my assurances, just think: *"What if she is right?"* And do it anyway. You have nothing to lose and everything to gain. You can only know for certain if you do it for yourself. Nobody else can do this for you and you alone will decide if reading this book and completing all the exercises was worth the time and money you invested.

Complete the following statements or write your own affirmations.

I enjoy being ____________________________________.

I love having ____________________________________.

I am proud of my ________________________________.

I feel ____.

I am ____ .

I am ____ .

I love ____ .

I delight in ____________________________________ .

I gladly ______________________________________ .

I easily ______________________________________ .

I joyfully _____________________________________ .

I am ____ .

I enjoy having __________________________________ .

I love being ____________________________________ .

I am ____ .

I have _______________________________________ .

Continue writing more affirmations for the characteristics or skills you want to develop further in order to reach a greater sense of fulfillment, achievement, joy, confidence, happiness and balance.

The following are some sample affirmations for you to help clarify the process of creating positive statements.

Affirmative – describe what you do want, rather than what you don't want:
"Connecting with prospective clients excites me."
"I enjoy organizing my time and activities effectively."

Emotionalized – include "feelings" – words that have meaning to you on an emotional level.
"My work is my joy."
"I am proud of my natural …pounds and I feel fantastic." (ideal and realistic weight goal)

Personal inclusion – "I" must be an integral part of the affirmations.
"I love my beautiful eyes."
"My …skills are strong and effective."

Present tense – clarity of behaviour and excellence, right now.
"Today, I am the best I can be."
"I enjoy meeting and speaking with people."

Specifics – identify exactly what you want to accomplish.
"Smiling at strangers each day gives me great joy."
"I easily contact …# of prospective clients each week."

Comparison – only with your best self.
"I attract wealth into my life."
"I am a well-prepared, goal-oriented and people-minded person."

Practical – use realistic standards such as "consistently", "regularly", rather than inflexible or perfectionist ones (always, every time…)
"I consistently enjoy my family one weekend per month."
"I regularly enjoy pampering myself."

Positive – add as many positive adjectives and characteristics as you can think of.
"I joyfully solve obstacles creatively."
"I love money and it loves me."
"Saying my affirmations is exciting and energizing."
"I like myself and generously share my gifts and talents."

Now that you have written confirmation of who you really are and what you believe to be true on a conscious or subconscious level, it is time to put your efforts to good use. It is time to take specific, positive action.

"Ideas without actions are worthless."...Harvey Mackay

ONE STEP AT A TIME

Living in a fast paced society, I know that most people want to see positive results quickly. To accelerate this learning process, you will want to involve as many of your senses as possible.

Sense of touch: Hand-write all your affirmations on a sheet of 8 x 11 1/2"paper. Make sure you write as clearly and as neatly as you can.

Sense of hearing: Say the affirmations out loud, as you are writing them onto the paper.

Sense of smell: Be aware and focus on the aroma of the paper and the ink you are using, while you are writing your declarations.

Sense of sight: At your earliest opportunity make several photocopies of your affirmations and have the sheets laminated. Place these in plain sight in various areas of your home, office, car and in your briefcase or purse.

Now, you are indeed ready to transform your life. Habits, good or bad ones, are established within 28 days. You are about to create a wonderful new habit of encouraging yourself and building belief in a better life and a confident new you. For the next month, use the same daily affirmations without fail. Upon rising, mid-day and before drifting off to sleep say your affirmations out loud, vividly imagining what it looks like to be or have what you are affirming. Feel the emotions associated with those positive images. The following is your daily routine:

- As you awake in the morning, before getting out of bed, read your affirmations out loud. Let each statement sink into your being and feel the sound of your voice reverberating through every cell of your body. Focus on the positive visuals coming into your mind and recognize the pleasant feelings these will bring forth. Take a deep breath and enjoy drinking in the positive energy you are creating. This is the process for all of your affirmations.

- While standing under the shower, imagine that the water washing over you represents all of the blessings you are enjoying in your life. For at least five minutes, as you are cleansing your body and washing your hair, remind yourself of all of the people, things and circumstances you can be grateful for each day. Even when you don't have the perfect job, you do have a job which gives you the money you need to take care of your lifestyle today. Maybe your relationship with your spouse could be more fulfilling, yet you do have somebody in your life you get to build a relationship with and so on. Some of the things that we can all remind ourselves to be grateful for and recognize as blessings (even though they may need improvement) are: shelter, family, friends, work, birds singing, animals loving us unconditionally, snow, butterflies, trees, bees, heat, clean water, children, neighbours, blue sky, the sun, opportunities in life, flowers, music, books to read, fresh air, movies to watch, people to meet, peace and freedom. These are just some of the blessings that come to my mind each morning. I remind myself of these and soak them into my being, cleansing my mind, while cleansing my body.

- As you are leaving the house in the morning, rather than the usual rushed goodbyes, bless your loved ones, wishing them a great and exciting day. My business mentor, Francine Hoffman, leaves her home every morning by calling out to her family "It's show time". We create our own excitement and set the tone for the kind of day we are going to have with these early morning rituals. Raising our own expectations of ourselves and our environment will have a positive impact on our life experiences.

- At mid-day speak your affirmations again, with enthusiasm and conviction, absorbing the vivid images and positive feelings associates with those, while breathing each one into your inner being. You are now reinforcing the positive tone you had created in the morning. Any negatives that popped up at work are being balanced out, reducing stress and anxiety while raising hope, increasing joy and a sense of calm.

- Before drifting off to sleep, repeat the affirmations again, allowing your subconscious mind to focus on the positive statements of fact. Vividly colour the mental pictures, internalizing the positive emotions associated with them, so that your conscious mind and body can embrace them as you rest through the night. Consistently reinforcing words, pictures and emotions over a period of one month brings about positive changes in your outlook on life, how you see and feel about yourself – thus empowering you to take appropriate actions, moving you closer to your big, huge and audacious goals.

The following three-pronged approach, affirming who you are, is a proven and effective process:

- Read your declarations out loud. This has a 10% impact on your subconscious mind and thoughts.

- Vividly picture in your imagination the change or the end result you want to create. This has a 45% impact on your subconscious mind and thoughts.

- Feel the emotions associated with your affirmations. Constructive imagination builds confidence and belief, impacting our subconscious and our thoughts with an additional 45%.

We have been affirming all of our lives and will continue to do so forever. The new awareness is that now you will choose what it is that you wish to affirm and have the tools to do so effectively. As explained in the three-pronged theory above, just saying the words is not enough. They alone have only a small impact on your thoughts. Yet, when you say those same words with feelings of excitement, positive energy and belief while visualizing the appropriate images to accompany them, then you are creating a powerful vehicle for change.

I certainly know that, in the past, I was able to affirm myself into a state of sadness in record time. I believe that many people are doing this without realizing that they are the creators of their own misery. Positive affirmations are a way to deliberately control the information you allow to control your own thoughts. You may wonder if this is a form of mind control and I would say yes it surely is! You get to be in charge of controlling the thoughts in your own head and what you choose to believe to be true about yourself. Our subconscious mind does not know the difference between the truth, a lie or a joke. It only knows that it has to bring to fruition any information that is accepted by us. Having seen ourselves in a negative light for some years, we are now using positive affirmations which are likely to cause a conflict in our subconscious mind. Initially, as you are repeating them daily, the "yeah, buts…" will pop into your head loud and clear. This is the subconscious saying, "Wait a minute! This is not in line with what you have been doing and saying for years". Thus, we have created conflict. Our mind's job is to resolve conflict, keep us sane and safe so we can operate and behave appropriately, living up to our own expectations and beliefs that we have programmed into our minds for years. I encourage you to get as many of your natural senses involved in the affirmation process and to repeat your declarations three times a day for at least one month, because we have to aggressively convince ourselves (the subconscious part of our mind) that this truly is who we are now. Once a conflict has been created, the subconscious needs to be clear about what it is now to bring into your reality. Once convinced by consistent affirmations, it will allow you to become aware of opportunities needed to create this life. President Abraham Lincoln said: *"Most folks are about as happy as they make up their minds to be."* Henry Ford said: *"Whether you think you can or think you cannot, you are right."* Napoleon Hill said: *"What the mind can conceive and believe, you can achieve."*

If you think that these men know something about success and the human experience, won't you too conceive the idea that you truly deserve to live your big, huge and audacious goals? If you can imagine it, see it and believe it through affirmations, then you can achieve it by taking the appropriate and effective actions. At this time, you might be hearing the *"yeah, buts..."* screaming in the recesses of your mind with such seductive statements as: *"Yeah, but... I am too old to change"*, or *"too tired everyday to add one more thing to my schedule"*, or *"too difficult"*, or *"too time consuming"*, or *"too silly"*, and *"can't teach an old dog new tricks"*. This is a normal response whenever change is introduced or suggested. The question I would like you to answer is: "If you keep doing what you have been doing so far, will the epitaph on your gravestone say – "Died at 35 years of age, buried at 87 years of age"? The price for living a life of low expectations, a life of mediocrity, is high. Are you paying the price for mediocrity or the price for excellence?

We all will be paying a price either way. There are no savings to be realized. The only difference is in the outcome. What do you choose?

"A bad habit never goes away by itself. It's always an undo-it-yourself project."...Abigail van Buren

PAYING THE FARE

All of us pay a price for the choices we make. Some of us are consciously aware of this fact and some realize this truth when it is too late to change the path of life.

In May of 1980, a frantic phone call from my mother caused me to jump on a plane and fly home to Germany. My Dad was 63 years old and dying. It was hard for me to believe that a man who had always been the picture of health, a man proud of his athletic build, could have suddenly taken ill and lay dying. Other family members assured me that I had come for no good reason, but my mother was hysterical. The moment I laid eyes on my dad in his hospital room I could sense the presence of death around him. His doctors confirmed this and decided, since I was going to be home for the next two weeks, they would release him so he could die at home.

One day, while I was sitting by his bedside, dad talked about how, if he were twenty years younger he would visit me in Canada again and travel with me to the Yukon and the North West Territories. My dad loved travelling, especially to quiet places. Born during the First World War, he grew up with little food and was four years old before his legs were strong enough to carry his small frame. Barely nineteen years old, World War Two started and he had to go to war. A peace loving, gentle boy was sent to kill the "enemy". Instead, his plane was shot down. The pilot was his best friend. Realizing that both of his legs were gone, the pilot decided to take his life with his own pistol. He made dad promise to never tell his mom. Dad never told. What a heavy burden for a young man to carry for so many years! After the war, my parents took over grandma's business - a restaurant - and with dad's talent as a great butcher and cook and mom's friendly personality, they soon established themselves as successful entrepreneurs. Though they never really lived up to their own potential, they made a comfortable living. Finally, we were able to go on family vacations. Dad always preferred quiet places. Too many people made him nervous, invading his peace of mind, destroying his communion with nature.

All of this was flooding through my mind as I was sitting by his bedside while he lay dying. I asked my dad, if he could live his life over again, what he would change. His answer surprised and deeply saddened me. "Everything", he said. He would have taken more chances and not been so afraid of what other people thought or of his own ability to succeed. I had never heard anything quite as sad in all my life. That day my dad gave me the greatest gift he could have ever have offered me. Fear of failure and regret take a heavy toll, a price too high to have to pay for "playing it safe" and settling for "good enough". Helen Keller said: *"Life is either a bowl of cherries, or it is nothing at all."* Are you prepared to pay the price for the life you 'get to live' if you do not start living, with passion, the life you deserve to enjoy? A price will have to be paid either way. You get to decide what will be written on your gravestone. I hope mine will say:

"She took many chances, gave generously, loved dearly and succeeded to live a life of passion with joy and enthusiasm. She walked her talk and made the world a better place."

WHAT WILL YOUR EPITAPH SAY?
WHAT WOULD YOU LIKE IT TO READ?

CHAPTER 5

Living your big, huge and audacious goals would conclude with a satisfying epitaph about your life that lets the world know you made the most of the sliver of time we call our life.

CHANGE, THE ONLY CONSTANT IN LIFE

Recognizing what you would have to do differently is not as important as identifying why you would want to make a change at all. Your 'why' needs to be crystal clear in your own mind, for without this clarity there can be no lasting or powerful change.

"When I first open my eyes upon the morning meadows and look out upon the beautiful world, I thank God that I am alive."
...Ralph Waldo Emerson

VISIONS OF PERSONAL SUCCESS

Most of you reading and working through this book live a pretty good life. You know from past experiences that change can be challenging, forcing you outside of your comfort zone. Further, your change may not be welcomed by some of the people closest to you. Remember being introduced to a new subject in school? In the beginning, the problems seemed overwhelming because you did not know how to arrive at the right answer. You did not understand the process... yet. At first you may have felt overwhelmed by the complexity of it all, fearful of not measuring up and, worse yet, looking foolish. But as soon as you "got it", the challenge disappeared, fear dispersed and you settled into your newly defined comfort zone. Before you had a chance to become comfortable in this new zone, the teachers would introduce the next challenge, and on it went from there. You do remember this, right? See? You already have plenty of experience in recreating new comfort zones, so this project will be a familiar one for you! There is nothing to worry about.

When you start changing your beliefs and opinions about yourself, you may find those closest to you are not being as supportive as you would have expected them to be. This is what I like to refer to as "The Mexican Crab Syndrome". Fishermen who catch these crabs place them in pairs in a woven basket without any lid to keep them confined. A single crab would easily climb out of the container and escape, however when two crabs are confined, they keep each other in check. As soon as one tries to make its escape, the second one will pull it back into the basket as if to say "Get back to where you belong".

Our friends and loved ones can act like Mexican crabs because any change on our part inevitably will cause a change for them as well. Be prepared to hear their "sage" advice, such as *"Why set yourself up for failure?"*, *"Be happy with what you have!"*, *"Remember, you tried something like this before and it just does not work!"*, *"This positive thinking stuff does not work for people like us, it just sells books and makes others rich!"*, *"Keep both feet on the ground!"*, *"Who do you think you are?"* and so on.

Therefore, be clear about your own reasons for why you want to pursue your big, hug and audacious goals. Share them only with those you are certain will encourage and support you – at least until you have built up a strong expectation within yourself through positive affirmations and creative visualizations.

Now that you understand why it is crucial that you are clear about your reasons for change, write down your personal reasons for change and the benefits this will bring into your life.

Personal reasons and benefits for changing: What is in it for you?

The reasons why you want to accomplish any goal is the powerful fuel you will need to keep the fire of your desire for success burning hot and furiously. How to accomplish your big, huge and audacious goals now is just a matter of implementing the appropriate tools and staying on your path to a successful life.

"Bright people learn from their mistakes,
brilliant people learn from other people's mistakes."
...Jonathan Weaver – Peak Performance

EMPOWERING CHOICES

Develop a dream board.
Paste images, pictures and phrases representing your big, huge and audacious goals onto a 2' x 4' bristle board. Be creative and have fun. This project will be a constant visual reminder of your reasons for committing to change your life. Remember, your mind is like a 'smart' missile looking for its target, and it is visually oriented. It will lock onto pictures effortlessly and focus easily and quickly on accomplishing goals that are visually depicted.

Keep the dream board where you can see it each day. Take photos of it and carry them with you wherever you go. Have photos in your briefcase or purse, on the sun visor in your car, in your wallet and on your office desk. Surround yourself with your goals, so that your subconscious can take in the consistent reinforcement, bringing your dreams into your reality quickly and easily.
Surround yourself with visual reminders of the things that you will have, how you will look and how it will feel when you have reached your goals. Part of your dream may include being healthy and fit, looking absolutely stunning and confident. Find a picture in a magazine showing a person that has these qualities. Cut the picture out and replace their face with a picture of your own. You are getting the idea, right? Have fun and enjoy the process.

Affirmations
Read them out loud at least three times a day with enthusiasm and gusto. Whenever you feel low on energy, repeat them again and again. Remember, there are many Mexican crabs in our lives. They may have

your best interest at heart, yet they can extinguish the fragile flicker of hope pretty quickly if you let them. Protect yourself against others and your own "yeah buts" by repeating your affirmations as often as you need to each day.

Initially, when I decided to include the affirmation: "I am a beautiful and confident woman" into my ritual, I simply could not get the words past my lips. I remember standing in front of my bathroom mirror, making eye contact with myself as I said my affirmations. Tears streamed down my cheeks, my stomach was tied into knots and anger welled up inside me as I struggled with the "beautiful" affirmation. So I took baby steps and started affirming something that I thought was beautiful about this 275-pound person. I liked my eyes and began there, affirming something I could believe was beautiful about myself. Better to take baby steps than get stuck. Do what you need to do to get started then gradually broaden and expand your affirmations. You are worthy and deserving of investing in yourself - creating the future you desire. I am living proof of the power of positive affirmations.

Blessings

Become aware of the many blessings already in your life. Even Mexican crabs can be blessings because they tend to care about you and want to keep you safe. Appreciate them for who they are, yet be cautious of their powerful influence.

Visualize

Take time to visualize your big, huge and audacious goals in as much detail and as vividly as you can, every day. This will cement your desire to continue the process and build belief that you can achieve.

Thoughts

Once in a while you may be faced with a set back. Recognize it is all temporary and doesn't represent failure. As long as you don't quit, you can succeed. If you should hear yourself saying or thinking: *"There I go, I knew I couldn't do this...." "I am such a failure..."*, immediately counter this by saying *"Stop"* while raising your right hand. *"This time I am succeeding, this is just part of the process".* Take control of your thoughts so they will take you where you want to be.

Courage

Know that courage is not the absence of fear. It is the mastery of fear. By that I am referring to your willingness to move forward and do what has to be done in spite of the fear. The word F.E.A.R. stands for False Evidence Appearing Real. Most of the things we are afraid of are figments of our own imagination- just proving how powerful a tool our imagination can be. When faced with fear, ask yourself what the worst thing that could possibly happen might be? You may find the worst is not really that horrendous and usually does not come to pass anyway.

Enthusiasm

Pursue your goals with enthusiasm, get excited about where you are going and enjoy the marvelous journey you are now embarking upon. When the spirit of enthusiasm really gets a hold of you, others around you will be drawn into your presence and eagerly offer support.

Find a mentor

Many successful individuals gladly mentor those who are willing to succeed, eager to do what it takes and ready to change. Find a person who has already reached the level of success you are goal setting for and ask them under what circumstances they would be willing to mentor you. These are not business coaches who need to be paid for their valuable services. These are successful individuals who may agree to take you under their wing and guide you if you can convince them that you are sincere about your dreams. Let your enthusiasm show and be prepared to learn, grow and change.

Giving back

The universal principle, 'you reap what you sow', is certainly one principle that every truly successful person I have ever met believes and lives by. The universe is energy, just like our thoughts are, and we attract to us that which we think about, believe and practice. I strongly encourage you to start giving for what you have already been blessed with and continue to do so while you are going through the process of reaching for your big, huge audacious dreams. I am not just suggesting you give financially. That is easy and the '10% tithing rule' applies here as it does for giving of our time and energy. If you don't yet have a worthy cause you want to support, finding one will not be a challenge. Give of your time and energy by mentoring others who are looking for your support, or volunteering your time at the food bank, senior home, etc. Sow that which you want to reap and do so with joy in your heart and a smile on your lips.

Success or failure really is a six inch job - that is the average space between our ears. This is to say, it is an inside job. You and I determine our life experiences by the thoughts that form our belief system. So, we determine our attitudes and based on those, we take actions. Therefore, you want to get control of your thoughts, because this will change your belief system, thereby developing positive attitudes and empowering you to take appropriate actions with confidence and enthusiasm. You can then confidently declare: *"That is just like me"* and it will be the absolute truth.

CHAPTER 6

MAXIMIZING THE AUTHENTIC SELF

Making a good first impression sets the tone for how others will treat us. Most of us learned that lesson from our parents when we were very young. We have been told that we only have one chance to make a first impression and if we miss that opportunity, we will have to work harder on establishing a positive rapport with others.

"You can't consistently perform in a manner that is inconsistent with the way you see yourself."...Zig Ziglar

IMAGE IS PERCEPTION

We have between seven and fifteen seconds to make a positive first impression. During those precious seconds of a first time encounter, others on a subconscious level, decide:

If we are:

- Professional
- Competent
- Intelligent
- Trustworthy
- Honest
- Nice

How can anyone make such important determinations in such a short period of time? If this is the question that popped into your head right now, you are not alone. I thought exactly the same thing when I first became aware of this information. We might think that it is rather shallow to judge others strictly by their image. We may ask if 'who we are as people' is not more important than the clothes we wear. I would certainly agree that the character of a person is of value to me and their image is not as important. Yet, we want to realize that those first impressions are not based on a conscious decision-making process but rather on primal instinct or gut reaction.

To understand this, we need to travel back in time to our ancestors, the cave men. In those days, men had to decide very quickly if a stranger approaching from afar was a friend or foe - if they needed to defend themselves against or embrace the newcomer. We have inherited this instinct and, while modern civilization prides itself on the progress it has made, our DNA still carries that powerful and subjective instinct, causing us to 'react' rather than respond logically to "newcomers". In this day and age of modern technology, we are communicating with one another at ever increasing speeds, using the latest tools available to us. Impressive Power Point presentations dazzle audiences and slick commercials sell products and services. Yet, eyeball-to-eyeball we are still governed by the caveman's imprint on our DNA. We know that, to succeed in business, we want to build relationships with our clients, suppliers and partners and that the best way to do that is by getting to know people in person.

When communicating with others, words only account for about eight percent of the message that we are delivering. Tone of voice is valued at thirty-six percent and visual presentation represents a whopping fifty-six percent of this equation. Effective communication has to take into account the visual we present to the world. In other words, our image.

What does your image communicate? Perception is reality, even though it may be flawed. Does your visual presentation convey an image of success? When you create a positive first impression of a successful and confident individual, you will be approached and accepted as such. I do hope the points I have made have convinced you that a positive image is of benefit to you in your business and career. The impact of our personal style through a powerful image also brings positive personal benefits. "Looking" the part tends to make us feel more confident in our own abilities and comfortable in our own skin. We intrinsically know when our image and who we really are inside are in sync. Then, we are presenting a congruent image to the world. We feel empowered, confident and successful. Projecting a positive image, conveying personal power, style and poise becomes your trademark, your brand. When you have accomplished this, you no longer have to feel self-conscious, worry about how you look or how you come across. You will know that who you really are is being communicated clearly and effectively to others. You can now give your undivided attention to those around you, making them also feel important and valued.

Identifying your personal style is crucial in determining how you can project your own unique image, your brand. Think back to a time when you attended a business event or private party and felt uncomfortable, ill at ease in your own skin.

What outfit were you wearing? ______________________________

Remember the colour of your wardrobe? ______________________

How did you style your hair? ______________________________

What specifically made you feel uneasy? ______________________

How did you act? ______________________________________

"Facts don't cease to exist because they are ignored." ...Aldous Huxley

FACTS ARE FACTS

How do you carry yourself when feeling ill at ease? Which of the following gestures would signal uncertainty to others? Check off the habits of yours (that you are aware of) that you might revert to when you find yourself in an uncomfortable situation. Do you….

- cross your arms?
- shuffle your feet?
- wring your hands?
- touch your face?
- play with your hair?

- avert your eyes, break eye contact?
- drop your shoulder?
- cock your head?
- cover your mouth?

Our bodies clearly communicate to the world how we really feel regardless of the words we use. Words of power and success may be spoken, yet our body language lets everyone know if these words are congruent with how we really feel. Sensing incongruent vibrations, the observer's defenses go up, distrust develops and consequently we are faced with results different from our expectations.

"When we were children, we used to think that when we were grown up we would no longer be vulnerable. But to grow up is to accept vulnerability... To be alive is to be vulnerable."...Madeleine L'Engle

BRANDING THE AUTHENTIC SELF!

We believe what we see, therefore perception is reality. Branding your own trademark – your powerful, unique style and authentic image – starts with understanding who you really are. In previous chapters you had the opportunity to identify and enhance your strength and inner character. This is who you really are; this is your authentic self. I have not yet met a person whose authentic self was less than terrific and I would think you are no exception. Knowing that you are a wonderful person on the inside, you want to project that for the entire world to see.

The people in our lives generally are quite eager to believe in us and accept us for who we really are. Most of us have, however, become masterful at sabotaging ourselves. Positive affirmations will pave the way for getting our own doubts and insecurities under control. Now, while you are working with your affirmations on a daily basis and building yourself up from the inside, let us have a look at how we can project the authentic self for the entire world to see, believe and accept as truth.

COLOUR

The importance of colour in projecting a positive, professional and authentic image became evident to me years ago just after I had been interviewed by a Vancouver television station. The session itself went well and I was excited to review the tape that I had made of the interview. I sat back in a comfortable chair and relaxed eagerly anticipating my first television performance. As the reporter directed a question to me, the camera swung around, and I could not see myself. It took my eyes a few moments to refocus and zero in on my image. I worn a nice business dress in what I believed to be an appropriate colour, yet it blended perfectly into the backdrop of the studio. At that point it became clear to me that my image needed a major tune-up. I set out to learn as much about image and colour as I could. I have since discovered that each colour has its own unique vibration and energy, evoking emotional responses from both the wearer and the observers.

The first visual the eye picks up on is colour. Therefore, the colour of your wardrobe, accessories and make-up is an important component in projecting a harmonious image of yourself. You may not realize which colour family is the best one for you. Here is a simple and very effective way to identify the colours that work best for you. Have people ever complimented you on how great you look, young, happy, energetic, etc? Maybe they asked you if you had been on holidays, lost weight or changed your hairstyle. Yet, you had done none of those things. Chances are that in that situation, you were wearing colours that really suited you. (This is different from a situation where someone has complimented your wardrobe itself or the colour of your outfit specifically.)

What were you wearing when complimented? ____________________

How do you feel when you wear this outfit? ____________________

What other colours would work for you? ____________________

If you are not sure, drape different colours under your chin; stand in front of a big mirror in a well lit room. The right colour for you will let your skin tone look more even toned, smooth and light. Your eyes will tend to sparkle and look brighter. Little lines and shadows will be less visible than before.

There is a harmonious flow from your natural hair colour to your skin tone into the colour draped under your chin. If you enhance your hair colour, you would of course cover it up for this procedure. If your skin has a blue undertone, then you will find the cool colours with a blue base are good choices for you when choosing wardrobe, hair, accessories and make-up colours. Skin with a yellow undertone would benefit greatly from warm colours with a warm yellow base. Since colour has vibration and energy, it is important to identify if cool or warm tones are appropriate for you. Remember, the eye picks up colour first and if the colour is not harmonious then that disharmony is communicated to others. To project an image of confidence, harmony, balance and authenticity, colour is your best friend. For those of you who can't decide which colours really work for you, an image consultant will gladly help you to identify your season. During the ten years that I worked as an image consultant, many of my clients realized they had been wearing colours that conflicted with their natural colouring. Changing wardrobe, hair, accessory and make-up colours took years off their faces and added pep to their step. For those seriously interested in projecting an authentic image, invest the time and money and be willing to make the changes. You are worth the time, money and effort.

STYLE

Every person has their own unique style, their own brand. Some are daring and enjoy dressing outrageously, others like to dress head-to-toe, while some just want to feel comfortable and are not concerned with looks at all. Which category do you see yourself in? What is true about you?

Pretend that you are going to represent your company at a trade show. You know that if you wear certain shoes, though perfect with your outfit, you will be paying a painful price at the end of the day. Will you:

• definitely wear the shoes meant to be worn with this wardrobe.
• definitely wear a comfortable shoe.

If you choose to project the "right" business image, chances are you like to dress head-to-toe. If you are 5'6" and taller, you want your wardrobe to be coordinated, presenting a polished, refined and finished look of quiet elegance. Your best choices are conservative business suits in smooth fabrics and in a solid or subtle colour scheme. Women add flair and colour with accessories, such as scarves, shells or blouses. Men add flair and colour with ties and shirts. Jewelry is size appropriate, elegant and refined.

If you are taller than 5'9" and a bit more daring, you will want to make more of a fashion forward statement and do so with unique one-of-a-kind designs in your wardrobe and accessory choices. Please realize that your incredible style and your fashion confidence intimidates others. Tone it down a bit for business and wear a big smile, signalling that you are approachable.

For those up to 5' 4", you too enjoy the dressed up look, yet you need some movement and can break up a basic business wardrobe with colour. Your wardrobe has to allow you the freedom to show your energy and vitality. Express your fun loving nature with colourful tops such as blouses, shells, and scarves. Coloured shirts and ties will do the same for the men. Because of your shorter statue, you want to be sure that all designs in your wardrobe and your accessories are size appropriate.

Those of average height, around 5'6", with round facial and body features, wavy or curly hair, may be drawn to a soft look and feel to your wardrobe. Straight lines and bold colours are not really your taste. Instead, you may prefer to wear flowing lines showing off your shapely body frame and gentle colours that express your romantic nature. Keep in mind that business etiquette strongly suggests that seventy percent of a woman's body and ninety percent of a man's body must be covered to be dressed appropriately for business.

If you are in this category, you choose comfort over looks, therefore business suits are probably not your first choice. Mix and match wardrobe pieces are much more to your taste. Shirts, slacks, blouses, sweaters and jackets are your choices. Tie your look together with one or two accessories and you are presenting the authentic business look ideal for you. Men can present a sharp business image with dress pants, shirts and jackets. Your fabric choices would include natural fibers, such as linen and heavier weaves. Accessories include leather bands, wood, ceramics and native crafted jewelry.

<u>MAKING IT FLOW</u> – Finishing touches make the overall image work, creating a harmonious flow, projecting an authentic and comfortable image.

HAIR – a stylish and updated cut is essential for men and women, expressing your personality and communicating your brand to others. Regarding facial hair for men – thirty-seven percent of the population has an opinion on facial hair. If you are keen on keeping yours regardless, make sure it is neatly trimmed thereby enhancing your overall professional image.

MAKE-UP – in business, some make-up is expected because it completes the professional look. Blending colours well will enhance facial features without drawing attention to any particular colour, giving the impression of a natural, yet finished look.

ACCESSORIES – up to four pieces can be worn to enhance the image we want to project, one of them being the focal point, expressing our brand. More than that would be distracting. Your accessories should reflect your personality and be size appropriate. At 6' tall, wearing tiny studs as earrings would not add to or enhance my image. Instead, they would look odd, creating a disharmonious look.

This would be the order of importance for your accessories:
1. Earrings;
2. Watch;
3. Necklace;
4. Wrist band, rings or brooch.

Keep in mind, if the wardrobe itself has unique buttons or a colourful design, those would count as one of the four pieces. Accessories are to support and enhance the overall image, yet not take over the entire look. I like to use them to draw attention to my eyes, as they are the windows to the soul, where real communication takes place. Therefore, earrings are an absolute must for women in business. Men today are keen on decorating their earlobes as well, and depending on the industry you are working in, that might be fine. Keep in mind that, when in doubt, make the conservative choice. It is all about making a positive first impression, presenting an image of success that will work for you!

HOSIERY – choose colours from your seasonal palette that allow for a harmonious flow from hemline to shoes. Personally, I don't want to draw attention to my legs or make shoes the focal point of my image. I want attention directed toward my eyes, encouraging direct and effective communication. Men do well in choosing longer executive-style socks, pulled up to just under the knee, allowing for legs to be crossed without exposing naked skin.

SHOES – are a definite symbol of success. We invest time, energy and money deciding on the right wardrobe, accessories, choosing the best make-up and often forget about the shoes. Creating an overall image is a head-to-toe experience, thus includes shoes. A good quality leather shoe, polished and well cared for will certainly present an image that is completely congruent with your personal brand. Shoes do not need to be brand new or represent the very latest fashion, yet they need to be clean, polished and well cared for to enhance your overall professional 'Dress for Success' image.

For those of you eager for more specific information about your personal style, please consider seeking the expert guidance of an image consultant. They will save you time in identifying your authentic style. They will save you money in the long run by helping you purchase wardrobe pieces that will enhance your own unique brand, your trademark. Knowledge is power and putting that knowledge into action spells success. Creating a professional image is not a cookie cutter approach to 'Dressing for Success', where everyone looks identical, yet it is a tool allowing you to present your authentic self, your brand and trademark.

CHAPTER 7

GETTING TO THE POINT

"The words that enlighten the soul are more precious than jewels."...Hazrat Inayat Khan

POWERFUL WORDS

Babies start to speak before they are a year old. Their first words delight us and before long they speak in full sentences, quickly grasping the power of words. Eventually, we take their ability to speak for granted and do not give it much thought. Maybe this would be a good time to think about how words impact our lives. It is said that lack of effective communication is the root cause in failed relationships.

DID YOU HEAR?

When I first arrived in Canada in 1972, I had mastered very few words in English and soon became painfully aware of the power of words. Sometimes I would get the word, yet not be aware of the underlying meaning accepted by the general public. One of the choices the dictionary offered to describe intersection was the word "intercourse".

I will never forget the day that I took my Canadian driving test. The driving instructor, testing my skills before issuing the license, asked me what I needed to keep my eye on as we were approaching an intersection. So of course I told him that I needed to keep my eye on all of the intercourse that was going on! (And who knew that a pedestrian, though the word looked as though it had something to do with trains, actually meant people! He broke into a huge grin when I shared that bit of information with him.)

I knew I had said something wrong, yet did not know what that was. Making up for that embarrassing moment, I wanted to sound intelligent, using a fancy word from the dictionary when answering the next question, "What do you have to watch for at a cross walk?" Of course now that fancy word had escaped me so I came up with another one that sounded great to me and proudly answered, "You got to watch for all the peasants crossing the road." By now, the poor man could barely breathe. I am sure my test was extra long, because he probably had not laughed that hard in a long while. Mind you, I did get my license. To this day, I wonder how often he has told the story about 'the girl from Germany' to amuse his friends and family. Words are indeed powerful, especially when their meaning can be conveyed to and received by the listener as intended.

"Education is the ability to listen to almost anything without losing your temper or your self confidence."
...Robert Frost

Chapter 7

COMMUNICATION STYLES

Just as each of us has our unique clothing and personality style, so do we have our own unique style of communicating. We may be using words that everyone should understand but find that people's reactions to simple words we use are not in line with our intentions. Effectively communicating with others is quite an art form. Recognizing our own style helps in understanding ourselves and ultimately makes our communications with others more productive.

On a scale of one to ten, omitting the number five, would you say that you are more formal, doing the appropriate things, being in control and taking charge (10) or are you more inclined to be casual, spontaneous, unstructured and express your feelings freely (1)? Write down your number: ____ On a scale of one to ten, again, omitting the number five, would you say that you are a high profile person, taking charge, expressing your opinions, and are assertive (10) or rather a behind-the-scenes, reserved individual, accommodating and co-operative (1)? Write down your number: _____ Now plot your numbers into the following chart: see example

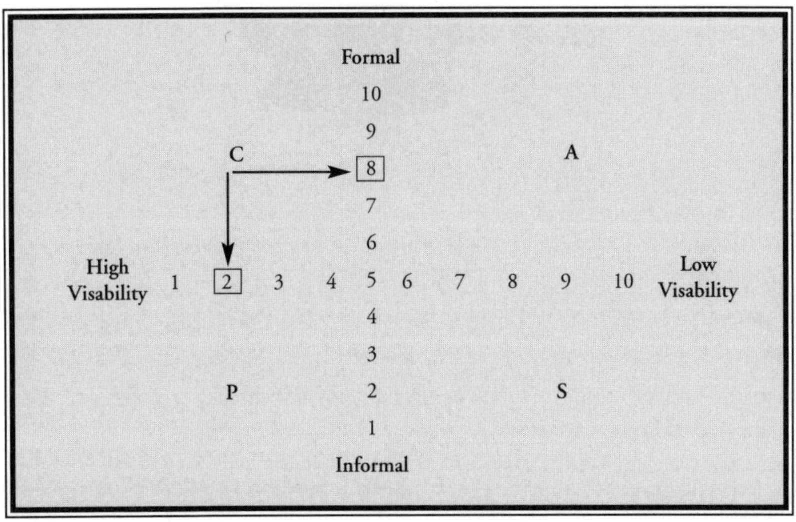

If you are more formal, giving yourself an eight and have a high visibility approach to life, disliking detail, rating yourself as a two, your chart would look as indicated above. You would mark the quadrant "C" as your preferred communication style. Of the many different tests available, this is a very simple and accurate tool of recognizing your personality style. Let's see if you can recognize yourself in the following descriptions. Remember, one personality style is not better than another, they all have strengths and challenges. They are just different, not better or worse.

"C" quadrant = Controller

Strengths:
Extroverted, optimistic, professional, correct, loves taking charge, results oriented, decision maker, born leader, loves saving time, dynamic, active, enjoys change, independent, self-sufficient, confident, goal oriented, practical, active, productive, enjoys opposition.

Challenges:
Needs to be right, compulsive worker, needs to be in control, can be impatient, perfectionist, seen as insensitive, resists advice, needs to correct wrongs, likes to tell others what to do, feels guilty when not productive, difficulties letting others into their lives.

"P" quadrant = Promoter

Strengths:
Extroverted, optimistic, flashy, colourful, loves attention and applause, appealing personality, talkative, storyteller, life of the party, witty and artistic, sense of humour, emotional, sincere at heart, demonstrative, enthusiastic, expressive, cheerful and bubbly, curious, charming.

Challenges:
Short attention span, great at getting started… can lack focus, talks too much, can be self-centered, disorganized and immature, tends to break commitments, promising more than they can deliver, seen as irresponsible and insensitive, are dramatic and emotional.

"S" quadrant = Supporter

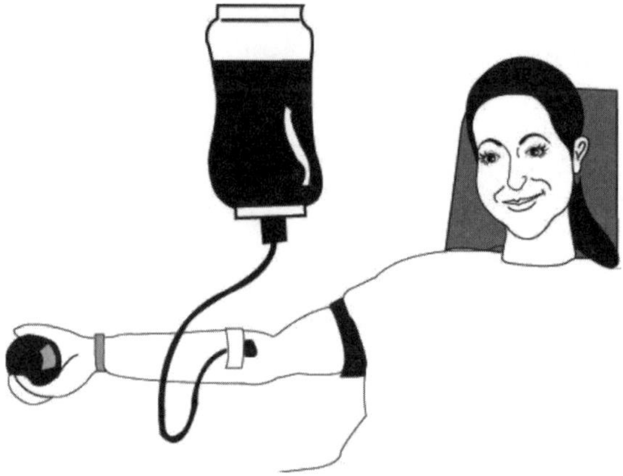

Strengths:

Introverted, comfortable and casual dresser, loves to help, sensitive, caring, sympathetic, kind, low-key, easy-going and relaxed, calm, cool and collected, patient, well-balanced, consistent, quiet, witty, competent and steady, peaceful and agreeable, mediates, good under pressure, inoffensive, good listener.

Challenges:

Lacks structure, gives negative feedback, lacks excitement, resists change, procrastinates, appears wishy-washy, difficulty saying no, can be pessimistic.

"A" quadrant = Analyzer

Strengths:
Introverted, thinker, proper dresser, loves data, facts, graphs and lists, creative problem solver, needs to make the right decisions, deep, thoughtful and analytical, serious and purposeful, finishes what is started, talented and creative, sensitive to others, self-sacrificing, conscientious, schedule-oriented, high standards, orderly and organized, economical, faithful and devoted, content to stay behind the scenes.

Challenges:
Slow at making decisions, lacks spontaneity, needs to save face, looks for the negatives, judges self harshly, procrastinates, seeks perfection in self and others, can be pessimistic.

One personality quadrant will be predominant, with a secondary influence, though you may recognize certain characteristics from the other two quadrants as well. It is important is to recognize your main quadrant and its secondary influence and how operating from there impacts your relationships with others. Usually, as long as you are communicating with someone from your own or a similar quadrant, nobody gets hurt and the relationship flourishes. Sometimes though, individuals from the same quadrants (such as my son Matthew and I) find it difficult to work and communicate effectively because they are just too much alike and grate at each other's nerves. However, we need the strengths of others from different quadrants to make things happen in our lives. As a 'promoting controller', I am quick to making decisions, focussing on the big picture, not the details, and doing it *now*. Yet I do need a solid foundation of facts and data to base my decisions on. Since I don't like doing that type of work it serves me well to have analyzers on my team, balancing my need for action with an organized and planned approach.

"The excellence of a gift lies in its appropriateness rather than in its value."...Charles Dudley Warner

SPEAK SO THEY WILL UNDERSTAND

Each quadrant personality sees the world through their eyes and communicates in their own unique manner. An outgoing and spontaneous personality style can strike sheer terror into the heart of a more reserved and logical person, just by the words used and the manner in which they are presented. The logical style will bore the outgoing personality to tears by insisting on presenting every last bit of data and facts collected. Creating fear or boredom in others will only result in ineffective communication, a problem just waiting for an opportunity.

Let us understand that each personality style is just fine; one is not better than the other. As a controller, I have the opportunity to remind myself of this fact regularly. My wonderful husband is a 'supporting analyzer', such a great combination, because we balance each other perfectly. However, I am sure that at times, I am too abrasive for his taste. But he is way too nice to ever say so because a supporter would not want to offend. Our first few years of married life were difficult though, largely due to the fact that I expected him to know what I meant to say, to be as excited about opportunities as I was and to talk about what was on in his mind, so we could share the experience and I could fix his challenges.

Questions that I asked him would just hang in the air. While no immediate answers were forthcoming, I would receive a beautiful and loving smile. My reaction to this was often fast and furious; surely it was obvious to anyone that he was playing a mind game with me! So, I would stop talking altogether! This nearly did me in, yet he seemed to be quite happy with this arrangement. After quite a long while I realized that he needed to digest the questions. Moreover, he loves to listen, so why ruin it all with an answer that I would dissect anyway? Our younger son, Alexander, is just like his dad and so over the years I have learned some patience, asking the questions and allowing for time to go by before looking for the answers. I have come to realize and appreciate my husband's strength, accepting that he will never be just like me and both of us are better off to be true to our own authentic selves. My husband has learned that I truly have a heart of gold and don't mean to cut people off at the knees. So he just loves me for the way I am, knowing that I am doing my very best to be as nice as I can.

Needing other people in our lives, it is important to become aware of their strengths and appeal to those strengths if we want to get cooperation (or just to be heard and understood). I encourage you to learn how to speak to and motivate individuals from different communication quadrants.

Controllers love to be in control, take charge and feel important. Speak to them at a faster pace, sharing your excitement for a vision or plan, leaving out boring details. Appeal to their natural talent for leadership. You can bet, when they get behind your plan they will get things done, delegating and inspiring others to pitch in and support your plan.

Promoters love to have fun and they desire attention and applause. Communicate to them with excitement in your voice, fast-paced speech, promising them a fun experience, leaving out all details and you will be sure to appeal to their enthusiastic personality. They will gladly tell everyone about your great idea with enthusiasm and charm.

Supporters love to be of assistance. They appreciate your calm request for help, pointing out how important their contribution will be to the successful completion of the project. Sincerity in your voice and an honest request for their input will be well received. They will be the calm center of any project, working quietly and steadily until the job is done.

Analyzers love to be recognized for their logical mind and appreciated for their ability to have lots of information. Honour this by presenting your plan of action calmly with plenty of data supporting the soundness of the plan. Give them a respectable amount of time before asking for their decisions. Allowing them time to think through their process is showing how much you respect their unique talents. They will make sure things are done right and on time in a conscientious manner.

Becoming aware of how to speak so that those around us really hear what we are saying is the most valuable tool I can offer you. The process of learning and then mastering any skill is a life long and valuable experience. The ideas presented are not meant to manipulate others or to poke fun at different communication styles. These ideas are meant to guide us toward more effective and satisfying communication.

It is my hope that you will honour those around you by accepting them as they are, valuing them and their strengths by learning to speak the language they can understand. Honouring and respecting those who are different from us is a true sign of self-confidence, good character and authenticity.

"Until one is committed, there is hesitancy, the chance to draw back, always ineffectiveness, concerning all acts of initiative. There is one elementary truth the ignorance of which kills countless ideas and splendid plans: that the moment one definitely commits oneself, then providence moves too. All sorts of things occur to help one that would never otherwise have occurred. A whole stream of events issues from the decision, raising in one's favour all manner of unforeseen incidents and meetings and material assistance which no man could have dreamed would have come his way. Whatever you can do or dream, you can begin it. Boldness has genius, power and magic in it. Begin it now."...Johann Wolfgang vonGoethe

CONCLUSION

Making a positive difference in my world is part of my mission in life. I hope this book has made a positive difference in your life and you are willing to continue your journey with the next work book in the "Get A Grip" series. "Get A Grip On Your Business" will be published in 2004. Remember the promise you made in the first chapter of this book? To answer all questions when they were presented to you. If you kept your word and filled in every space made available to you for your answers, then you have taken a hold of this wonderful learning experience and gained valuable insights into the unique person you really are. Welcome to your authentic self. You have honoured me with your commitment, honesty and determination. As I am only a mirror for you, let me say this: you have honoured your authentic self with commitment, honesty and determination. Congratulations!

FINAL THOUGHTS

"A journey of a thousand miles begins with but a single step." ...Chinese proverb

Everyone's journey through life is filled with great opportunities and amazing challenges, no exception. We may not be able to control our environment, single-handedly stop a war or boost the economy, yet we do get to choose how to interpret and react to what is happening in our lives. We can wish for great things to happen for us, yet that alone will not make it so. A price does have to be paid for every big, huge and audacious goal that we want to accomplish. There is no free lunch for anybody. Decide on your big, huge and audacious goal, take positive actions, hold on to your dream and believe that you deserve it, because you do. When you put the work and effort into a project, are committed to doing the work, determined to see it through to the end and willinåg to accept the occasional setbacks, you will succeed. The universe is just. Honest efforts are rewarded to the same degree that they were invested.

Remember to control your thoughts. Beware of what you are saying to yourself because that inner dialogue can build or destroy your dreams. Invest time and money into your greatest asset, yourself. Know that you are a precious gift to the world so let your light shine as you reach boldly out and connect with your very special and authentic self. Be good to yourself in thoughts and in deeds. Surround yourself with mentors who empower you, build you up and believe in your dreams. Life is a journey – make yours a wonderful and exciting one. "Get a Grip" on your uniqueness, your true and authentic self.

TRUE SUCCESS:

"To laugh often and much, to win the respect of intelligent people
and the affection of the children; to earn the appreciation
of honest critics and endure the betrayal of false friends;
to appreciate beauty; to find the best in others;
to leave the world a bit better, whether by a healthy child,
a garden patch, or a redeemed social condition;
to know even one life has breathed easier because you lived.
This is to have succeeded."...Ralph Waldo Emerson

ABOUT THE AUTHOR

Passionate about the power of positive thinking, Renate Weiler has successfully transformed the lives of numerous individuals by encouraging them to "Get A Grip" on their authentic self and live a more fulfilling and joyful life.

Renate is not just another "touchy-feelie, positive thinking, I'm okay you're okay, pull your own strings, motivational and inspirational speaker" but a survivor and mentor. For over twenty years Renate has walked her talk and empowered audiences to create the life they richly deserve.

As a sought after Keynote Speaker, President of Executive Mentors and Founding Managing Director for eWomenNetwork, in Canada, Renate touches many lives and enjoys mentoring others to "Get A Grip" on their success.

For Keynotes, Seminars, Interactive Workshop and One-on-One Mentoring availability contact Renate directly:

info@Renate-Weiler.com

Call 905-830-1985

For additional information, visit: www.Renate-Weiler.com

INTERACTIVE WORKSHOP OPPORTUNITIES

"Get a Grip" internalizing the strategies and activating the tools you have read about in these 3 1/2 hour sessions.

1. **Journey to Today!**
   Participants develop effective beliefs, powerful thought patterns and success attitudes, thereby facilitating positive actions now.

2. **Creating a Great Tomorrow!**
   Designing their own 'Great Tomorrow', individuals take quantum leaps forward by embracing accountability as a powerful point of view.

3. **Insights from the Journey!**
   Unleashing the beauty of the authentic self by controlling thoughts and tapping into the gifts within each person's mind.

4. **Getting From Here to There!**
   Developing sound and effective affirmations tailor-made for each participant, propelling them toward their own unlimited possibilities.

5. **Change, the only constant in life!**
   Proven success strategies, designed and developed by each participant and adopted into their daily routine ensures a greater sense of success, more balance and joy. Participants create their own unique 'Dream Board' - powerful tools in attaining desired goals.

6. **Maximizing the Authentic Self!**
   Individuals gain confidence and poise when understanding their own unique persona and how to enhance their image following simple steps and guidelines.

7. **Getting to the Point!**
   Participants learn how to recognize and interact more effectively with various communication personalities, taking the stress out of difficult relationships.